HORSES
How They Came To Be

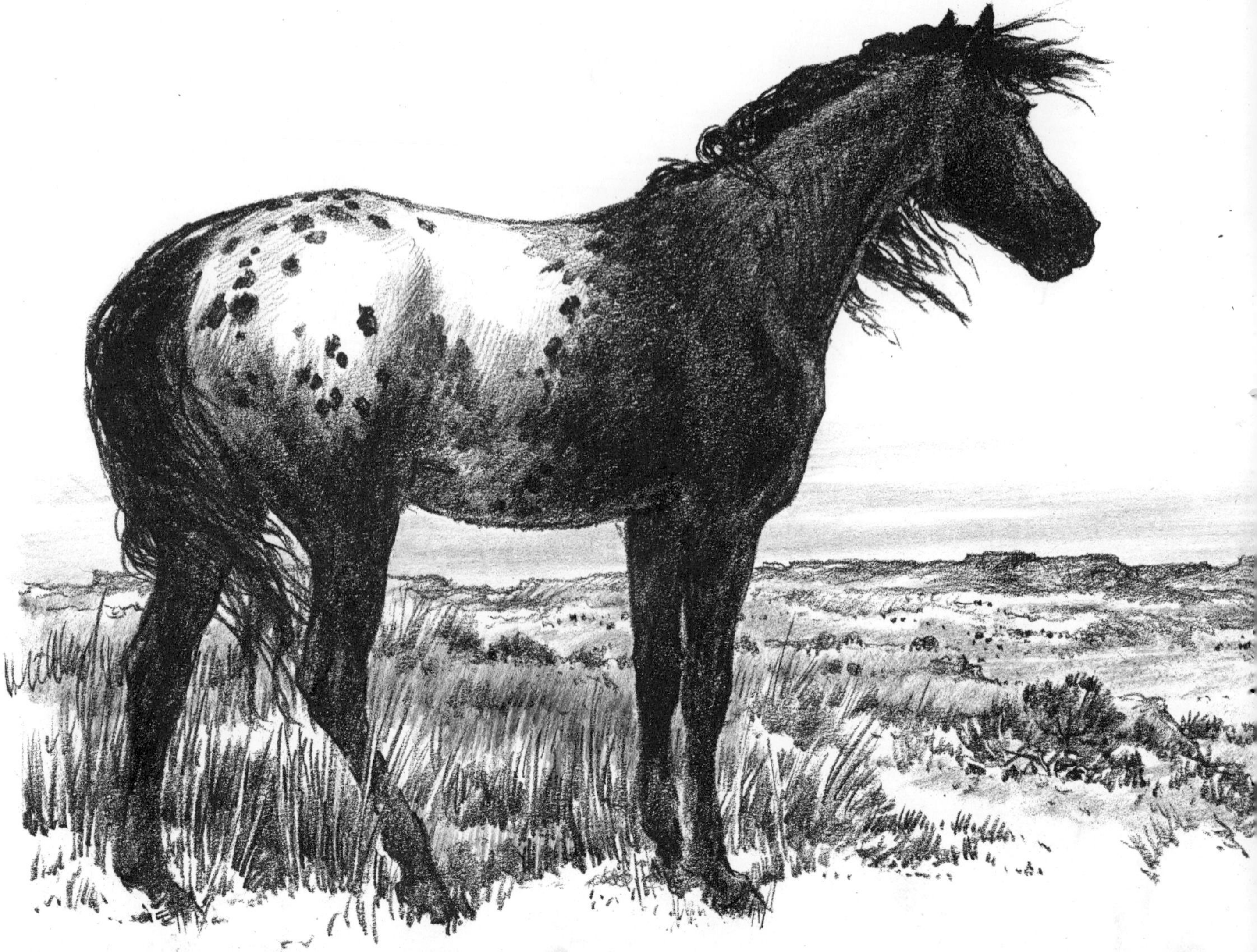

HORSES
How They Came To Be

JULIAN MAY

Illustrated by LORENCE F. BJORKLUND

HOLIDAY HOUSE · NEW YORK

Text copyright © 1968 by Julian May Dikty. Illustrations copyright © 1968 by Lorence F. Bjorklund. All rights reserved. Printed in the United States of America.

They were small and shy, the first horses in the world, and not much bigger than a fox. Their large eyes helped them watch for enemies. Their strong legs helped them run from danger.

HYRACOTHERIUM, 12 INCHES HIGH, LIVED IN NORTH AMERICA 60 MILLION YEARS AGO

The earth was warmer and wetter when the first horses lived. There were no people then. Most of the animals we know today did not live on earth either. Instead, the earth had other kinds of animals. The largest and strongest animals were the mammals—animals with furry coats that had live babies and nursed them with milk.

DROMOCYON

The small horses that lived sixty million years ago are given the name eohippus (ee-oh-HIP-us), which means "dawn horse." Some were only ten inches high. Others were as large as a collie.

We know about eohippus because scientists have found its bones, buried in the earth and turned to stone. These bones are called fossils. Many museums have fossil bones of the first horses.

Nobody knows what color the dawn horse was. We can only guess whether it was plain or spotted. But a scientist can tell from the bones how big the horse was and what shape it had. The teeth tell what kind of food it ate.

EOHIPPUS FOSSILS ARE FOUND IN WYOMING AND MANY OTHER PLACES

ACTUAL SIZE

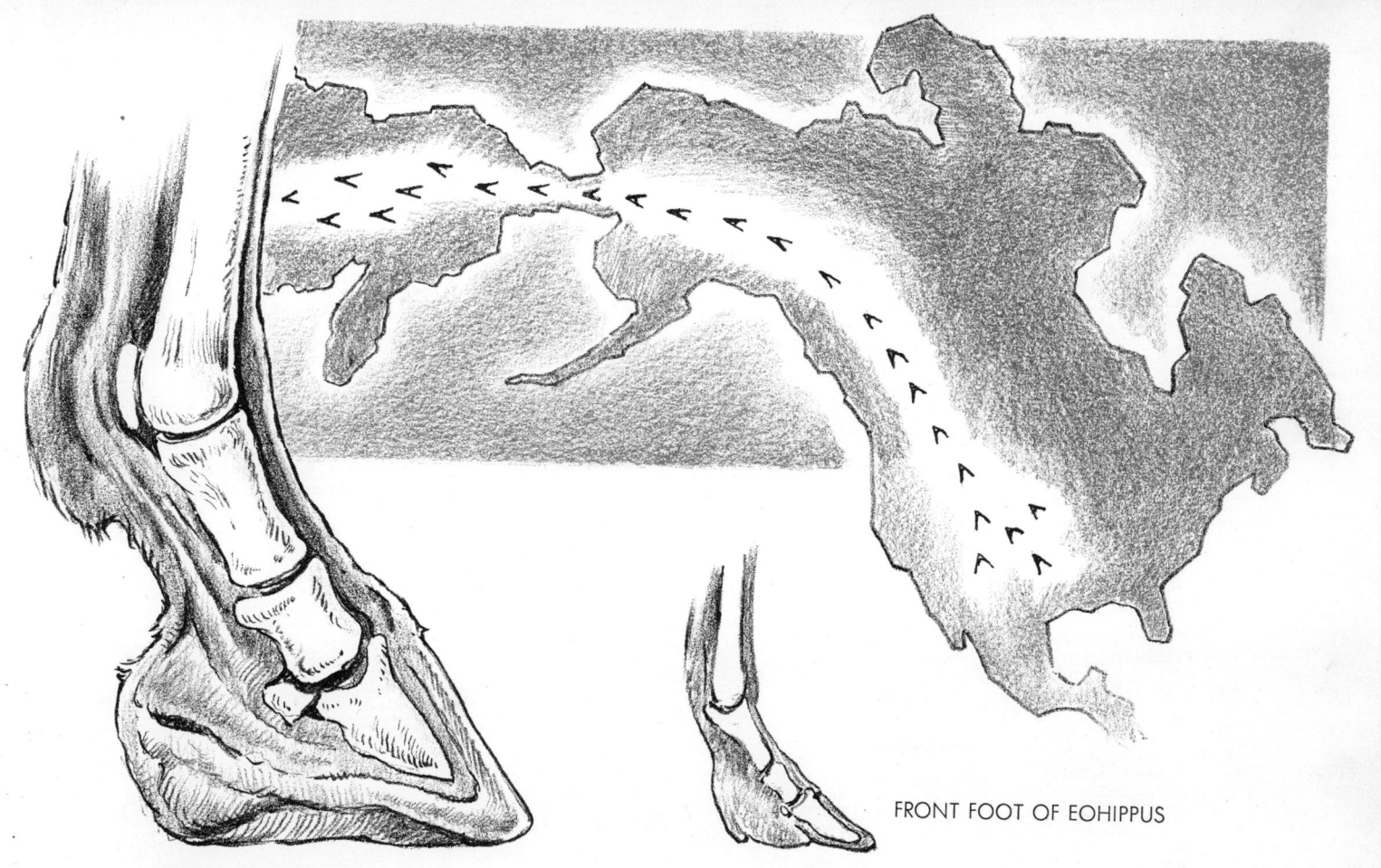

FRONT FOOT OF MODERN PONY

FRONT FOOT OF EOHIPPUS

Eohippus horses had four toes on each front foot and three on each hind foot. At the end of each toe was a tiny hoof. The little horses were found in many places around the world. They could travel from North America to Asia and Europe, because these lands were joined together long ago.

How did the eohippus come to live on earth?
Scientists tell us that new living things
always come from older ones. The dawn horses
had relatives that lived on earth much earlier.
They had short legs with five toes on each foot.

ECTOCONUS MAY HAVE BEEN
A LONG-AGO RELATIVE
OF EOHIPPUS

They could eat both meat and plant food. Babies were born to these animals and grew up. They had more babies, which also grew up. And each set of babies was just a bit different from their parents, just as you are different from yours.

SOMETIMES BABIES HAD LONGER LEGS THAN THEIR PARENTS. THIS HELPED THEM TO RUN BETTER

Sometimes the different babies changed
in a way that helped them live better.
Fast, slender animals with long legs
could escape enemies better. They did
not get eaten as often as the short-legged
kinds, so the long-legged animals had more
babies than the others. And after many,
many years, there were no more short-legged
relatives of the horse left.

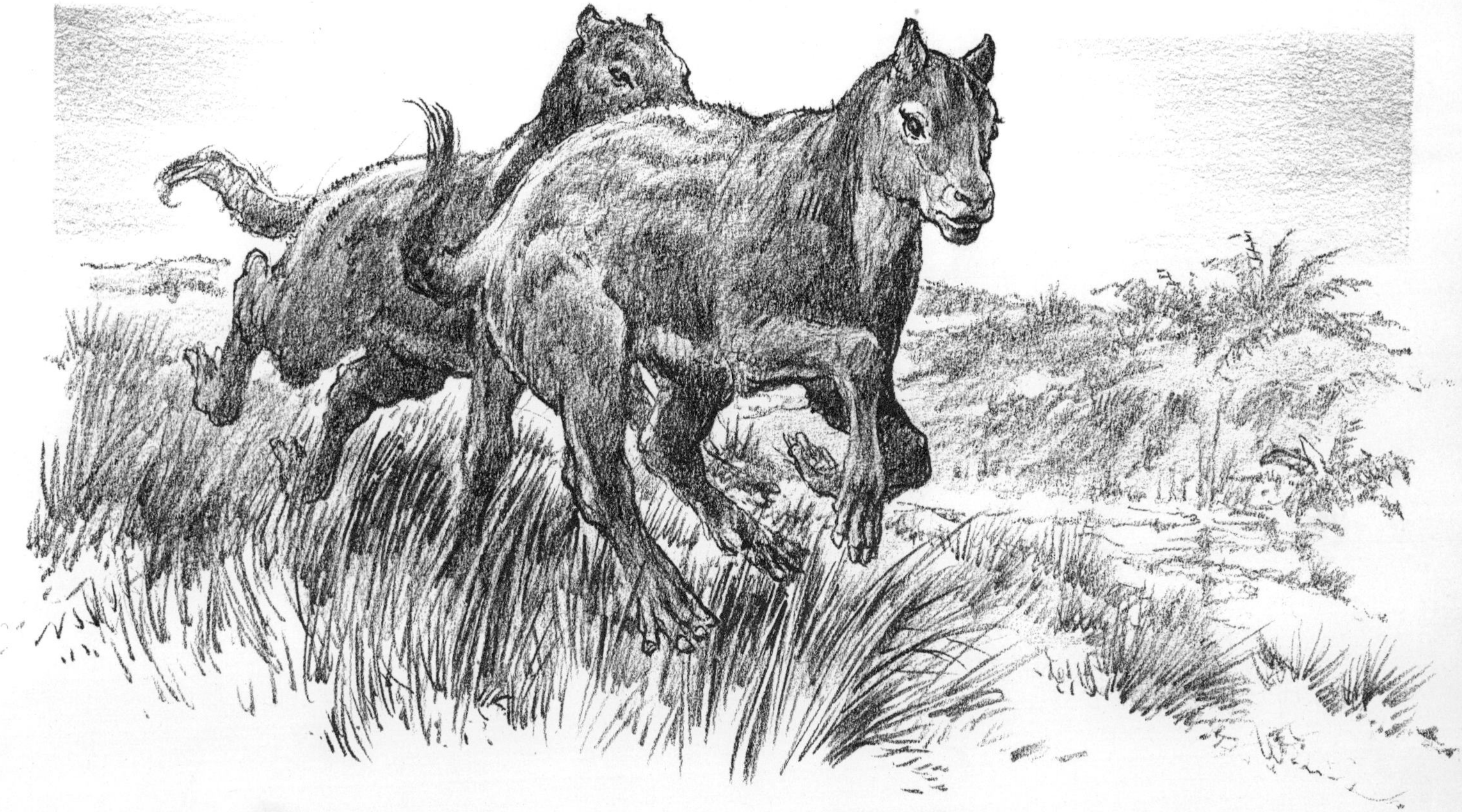

THE FIRST HORSES MIGHT HAVE COME TO BE IN THIS WAY

It took millions of years for the old relatives of the horse to change to eohippus. This slow change in living things is called evolution. All living things change slowly through evolution. The old kinds disappear and new kinds come into being. Life is always changing, always evolving.

Eohippus evolved too. In North America a new kind of horse appeared. Mesohippus (mess-oh-HIP-us) looked a little more like today's horses than eohippus did. It had three toes on each foot. The fourth toe on the front foot had slowly disappeared through evolution.

MESOHIPPUS LIVED ABOUT 30 MILLION YEARS AGO

Mesohippus was about two feet high at the shoulder—almost as big as a wolf. Scientists can tell from its teeth that it ate soft plants from the swamp or forest. Perhaps its spreading toes helped it move quickly through wet places.

Scientists have found and named many other fossil horses that looked much like mesohippus. Some of these horses crossed from the New World to the Old World and mated with horses there. Still different kinds of horses were born. These traveled wherever they could find food.

HYPOHIPPUS WENT FROM NORTH AMERICA TO ASIA

Food! It is more important than almost anything else to an animal. If there is enough food, animals will have many babies. They will be healthy. But if the food disappears, so will the animals that depend on it.

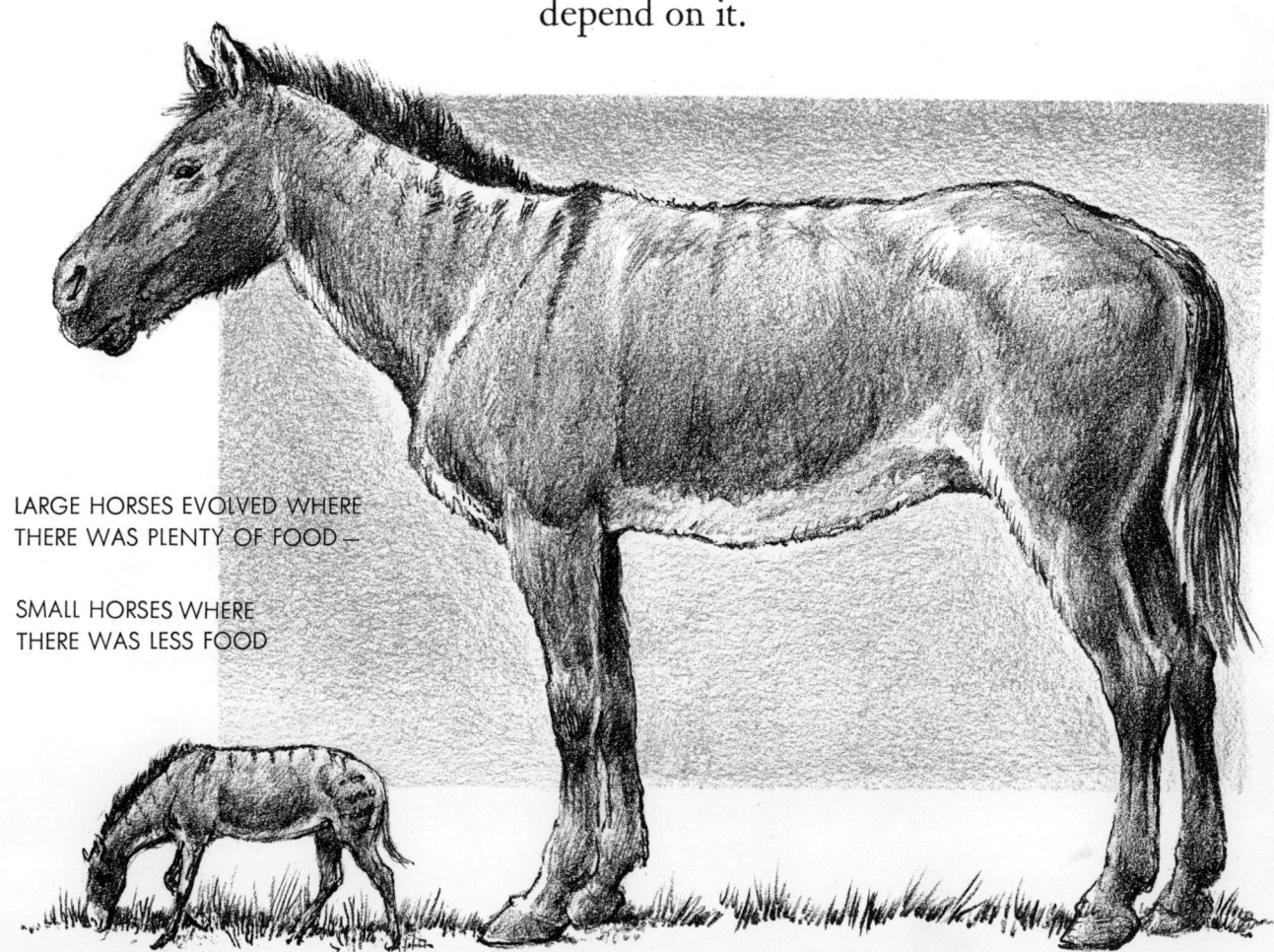

LARGE HORSES EVOLVED WHERE THERE WAS PLENTY OF FOOD —

SMALL HORSES WHERE THERE WAS LESS FOOD

ARCHAEOHIPPUS — 15 INCHES TALL

MEGAHIPPUS — 5 FEET TALL

About twelve million years ago, the earth grew drier. Soft, juicy plants that needed much rain could no longer grow so well. Instead, great parts of the earth became covered with grass. Horse babies that were born with teeth shaped a certain way could eat grass. But the horses that needed soft plants found little to eat.

MERYCHIPPUS, A THREE-TOED HORSE

After many years, the horses that needed soft plants disappeared. Only the grass-eaters were left. One of these was named hipparion (hip-PAR-ee-un). Great herds of these horses roamed North America, Asia, Europe, and Africa.

MACHAIRODUS WAS A SABER-TOOTH CAT
THAT ATTACKED HORSES

With plenty of grass to eat, the horses grew larger. And the meat-eaters that chased the horses grew, too. The meat-eaters also evolved. Horses had to run faster in order to escape. The horses that ran fastest were those whose side toes were smallest.

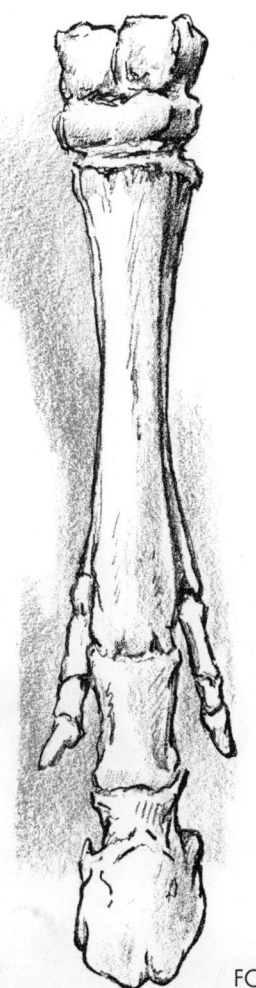

The horses that ran fastest lived longest, so they had more babies. As many years passed, young horses were born with smaller and smaller side toes. The large center toe on each foot carried the horse's weight. Pliohippus (ply-oh-HIP-us), a horse that lived in North America at the same time as hipparion, was the first real hoofed horse. It is the ancestor, or long-ago relative, of today's horses.

FOOT BONES OF HIPPARION

FOOT BONES OF PLIOHIPPUS

About a million years ago, the modern kinds of horses appeared in North America. Scientists call them equus (EE-kwus) horses. There were many kinds. But they all had a single toe on each foot, and their teeth were shaped much alike.

Equus horses spread all over the world—
to South America, Asia, Europe, and Africa.
Just about this time, the first men were
appearing. They must have seen the horses.
Perhaps they used them for food. But they
did not try to ride the animals.

Both men and horses evolved during the last million years. They moved about the earth. During the great ice ages, men came from Asia to North America. There they found and hunted vast herds of horses.

Men spread slowly from North America to South America, hunting horses and other animals as they moved. Today scientists find their spear points next to fossil horse bones.

CAVE MEN PAINTED THESE
HORSES AT ALTAMIRA, SPAIN

In Europe men lived in caves. They painted pictures and made carvings of the wild horses that they had hunted. We can still see these pictures today.

All during the ice ages, early men in North America hunted horses. But then, when the ice began to disappear, the North American horses vanished, too. What could have happened to them? Perhaps some strange disease killed them.

Perhaps man himself had something to do with the horses' disappearance. Scientists simply do not know what happened. But when the first explorers came to North and South America, they found no horses at all.

GRANT'S ZEBRA

QUAGGA

In the Old World, several horselike animals remained. Africa had zebras and the strange-looking quagga.

KIANG

The wild ass lived in Africa. Modern donkeys and burros came from these animals. Asia had another animal like a donkey, the kiang (kee-ANG).

ASS

The wild horse that was the ancestor of today's horses lived in Central Asia, in Siberia and China. The land there was dry but grassy. At some time, perhaps about 6,000 years ago, the people began to tame the wild horse and make it carry or pull things.

And then somebody discovered that men could ride horses. Men kept these tame horses and showed other people how to ride them. More and more horses were tamed.

All of the different horses that we
know today came from this one kind of wild horse.
Evolution did not bring about these horses.
Man did — by choosing which horses would be
mothers and fathers. This is called horse
breeding. After thousands of years, horses
could once more be found
all over the world.

SPANISH EXPLORERS BROUGHT
HORSES BACK TO THE NEW WORLD

Most wild members of the horse family are disappearing now. But tame horses will continue to be the helpers and friends of mankind for a long, long time.